A Family Matter

A Family Matter

A Guide to Organizing Your Personal Estate

William A. Verkest

Brown Books Publishing Group
Dallas

A FAMILY MATTER
Copyright © 2002 by William A. Verkest

Printed and bound in the United States of America.

All rights reserved.
No part of this book may be reproduced, stored in any retrieval system, or transmitted in any form or by any means, mechanical, photocopying, recording or otherwise, without permission in writing from the publisher; except by a reviewer, who may quote brief passages in a review to be printed in a magazine or newspaper.

Although the author and publisher have made every effort to ensure the accuracy and completeness of the information contained in this book, we assume no responsibility for errors, inaccuracies, omissions, or any inconsistency herein. Any slights of people, places, or organizations are unintentional.

For information please contact Brown Books Publishing Group
16200 North Dallas Parkway, Suite 170, Dallas, TX 75248
972-381-0009   www.brownbooks.com

First Printing 2003
ISBN 0-9725592-0-5
LCCN 2002094834

Dedication

To My Family:
Judy; David, Rachel, Cassie, and Alex; Stacey and Mike; and Todd.
And To Yours

Contents!

Acknowledgments!	ix
Welcome!	xi
Why!	xiii
Purposes!	xv
CHAPTER 1 – Principal Profile	1
CHAPTER 2 – Wills/Powers of Attorney	5
CHAPTER 3 – Investment Accounts	9
CHAPTER 4 – Financial Summaries	13
CHAPTER 5 – Retirement Statements	23
CHAPTER 6 – Insurance	27
CHAPTER 7 – Net Worth	33
CHAPTER 8 – Income Tax Returns	39
CHAPTER 9 – Open Accounts	43
CHAPTER 10 – Safe Deposit Box Inventory	49
CHAPTER 11 – Information for Personal Representative	53
CHAPTER 12 – Miscellaneous	69
Your Personal Red Book	73
Next!	77
Thanks!	79
Appendix – Formats and Spreadsheets	81
Biography	83

Acknowledgments!

I am pleased to acknowledge and express my sincere appreciation to Rick McVay, Attorney at Law; Steve Kleiber, CPA; and Judy Verkest who encouraged the development of this work. And also to the superb staff of the Brown Books Publishing Group, whose counsel and creativity added immeasurably to its presentation.

A Family Matter

Welcome!

Welcome to *A Family Matter*, a gathering of information capable of defining your future and the future of your family.

If you are head of a household, and are willing to accept the premise cited above, there are two critical tasks with which you must be involved.

The most important task for you to do, right now, is to concentrate on staying healthy (socially, physically, spiritually, and fiscally) so that you can live a long and happy life.

The second critical task for you to do, right now, is to organize your estate so that your family can make timely decisions during a life threatening situation, or upon your demise, settle your estate quickly, easily, and nearly worry free.

How you manage the first task is up to you. This GUIDE to organizing your personal estate (also called the Red Book) is designed to assist you in meeting the second task. All you need to do is commit yourself to some serious start-up hours and then maintain <u>your</u> personal Red Book, periodically.

NOTE: As I gathered my information suggested in this GUIDE, I put it into a red loose-leaf binder. It subsequently became known, simply, as the "Red Book." I have chosen to carry this reference throughout this GUIDE.

A FAMILY MATTER

TO USE this GUIDE and create your own Red Book,

    You will need: A large red three-ring binder
                              Tabbed dividers
                              Three-hole punch
                              Use of a copier

First, read this GUIDE through to understand the magnitude and scope of the project. Each chapter outlines the particular topic and information you will be gathering. Make as many copies of the forms/formats as you feel you will need, or create your own in a format with which you feel comfortable.

Label the tabs on the dividers as per chapter title.

As you assemble the documents, place into your personal Red Book behind the appropriate tab.

Why!

Why was the GUIDE developed?

On May 5, 1997, my mother died leaving me the singular responsibility of closing her estate. Certainly, her estate was not complex. But, I quickly learned, complexity does not diminish the enormous number of tasks to complete upon the death of a loved one. As with her estate, the tasks themselves were neither extremely difficult nor totally complex.

What was difficult was organizing everything to meet the many legal and procedural requirements detailing a lifetime of achievements. The only documents my mother left pertaining to her estate were a simple will, an unbalanced checkbook, and two typewritten pages of instructions.

The two pages showed bank account numbers, family and friends to notify upon her death, and the disposition of certain special possessions. Clearly better than nothing, but no where near the level of detail needed to ensure a timely close to her seventy-seven years.

Adding a measure of complexity was that my mother and I lived in different states, necessitating an attorney in the state in which she lived. Upon the recommendation of a trusted friend in that state, the service of an exceptionally talented (and patient) estate planning attorney was secured to make sure every detail was completed. Even her first counsel was reassuring when she said we should worry about the funeral arrangements while she worried about the start-up of necessary paper work.

Nonetheless, there was work to do—organizing my mother's estate.

As my wife, Judy, and I emptied endless drawers, boxes, files, and folders in search of tax records, places where my mother had done business, details concerning her lease and car, and even the location of the key to her safe deposit box, I told myself I would not let lack of organizing my estate be the focus of my family's attention upon my death.

In the GUIDE that follows, I have detailed the types of information the attorney asked for, through one request or another. With the exception of the will, everything had to be created or recreated following that exhaustive search through my mother's belongings. And, to this I have added information, readily available and essential, to the multiple purposes of this GUIDE.

What then are the purposes of this GUIDE?

Purposes!

Organization of your personal estate is the central purpose of this GUIDE. It will help you put in place the information that your family and/or your personal representative will need to carry-out the disposition of your estate as they would require during a life-threatening situation or upon your demise.

The second purpose of this GUIDE is to assist you in the management of your estate during your lifetime, tracking that important information in making ongoing decisions with regard to the management of your life's assets.

There is also a benefit during tax season. By following the GUIDE you will systematically put into place most of the information you or your accountant will need to expeditiously file your tax return each year.

And, not the lesser of any of those above, there is a certain peace of mind through the use of the GUIDE, knowing you have helped your family during what assuredly will be a most difficult time.

One other thought before you get started. Regardless of your age, you can employ this GUIDE now. The younger you are, the more lifetime benefit there will be. You can build each section as your assets grow and by keeping it current, its benefit to you and your family will be immeasurable during your life and, more importantly, immediately following it.

Good luck in the adventure ahead!

PRINCIPAL PROFILE

WILLS/POWERS OF ATTORNEY

INVESTMENT ACCOUNTS

FINANCIAL SUMMARIES

RETIREMENT STATEMENTS

INSURANCE

NET WORTH

INCOME TAX RETURNS

OPEN ACCOUNTS

SAFE DEPOSIT BOX INVENTORY

INFORMATION FOR PERSONAL REPRESENTATIVE

MISCELLANEOUS

Principal Profile

1

A Family Matter

1

Principal Profile

Tab 1 gathers basic information pertaining to the principals of the estate, typically husband and wife.

Information on children, siblings, and other family members may also be useful here. However, it can also be deferred until Tab 11, Information for Personal Representative.

This has significant value to your family should they have to respond to a life-threatening situation.

ACTION: Complete the information as shown, or desired, and place into your Red Book as Tab 1.

UPDATE: As required.

PRINCIPAL PROFILE

	Principal	Principal
Name		
Address		
Home Telephone Number		
Work Telephone Number		
E-mail Address		
Social Security Number		
Medicare Number		
Date of Birth		
Blood Type		
Allergies		
Health Issues		
Organ Donor (yes/no)		
Personal Representative (Executor/Executrix)		
Name		
Address		
Telephone Number		
Relationship		
Attorneys-in-fact		
Medical Power of Attorney		
Name		
Address		
Telephone Number		
Statutory Power of Attorney		
Name		
Address		
Telephone Number		

Wills/Powers of Attorney

2

2

Wills/Powers of Attorney

Tab 2 gathers what is perhaps the most important information your family can have in either a life-threatening situation or upon your demise.

It is suggested that a copy of the following (or similarly) titled documents be included in your Red Book. It is also suggested that you prepare only one original Last Will and Testament and two originals of the other documents. Keep an original copy of the latter documents at home so they can be accessed immediately upon need. File the original Last Will and Testament and the second originals of the other documents with your attorney or place them in a secure location such as a safe deposit box that is fire safe. It is also suggested that a copy of all documents be provided to your personal representative. Typical documents to include here are:

- Last Will and Testament:
  - Provides specific instructions on the disposition of your estate assets.

- Statutory Durable General Power of Attorney:
  - Delegates specific authority to act on your behalf to a specific person.

- Medical Power of Attorney for Designation of Health Care Agent:
  - Designates a specific agent to make all health care decisions on your behalf.

A FAMILY MATTER

- Directive to Physicians and Family or Surrogates:
  - Provides specific direction concerning your medical treatment should you not be able to make that decision

ACTION: Place a copy of the cited documents for both yourself and your spouse in your Red Book as Tab 2. Note where the originals of the documents are kept and/or who to contact to access them.

UPDATE: As your family situation changes; review at least annually with your attorney or other appropriate advisors.

NOTES:

- These documents are extremely complex, powerful and potentially dangerous. They should only be completed with the assistance of a qualified attorney. Use of do-it-yourself kits is strongly discouraged. Please remember, you are providing essential information to your family on how you want your life to be fulfilled.

- The titles of these documents are those used in the state in which I reside. Consult your attorney for the appropriate documents which meet your state's definitions.

- If you create nothing else suggested in this GUIDE, do this!

3

Investment Accounts

3

Investment Accounts

Tab 3 gathers statements and reports pertaining to your financial investments and holdings. It may include:

- Monthly brokerage firm account statements.
- Monthly/quarterly mutual fund statements.
- Quarterly annuity statements.
- Periodic diversification reports.
- Statements of recognized gains and losses.
- Monthly bank statements.

ACTION: Place these types of documents into your Red Book as Tab 3. Also, include the source document (application/signature card) which creates each of the cited accounts. The source documents will, for example, verify if the account is or is not a joint account, and whether or not there is a right of survivorship.

UPDATE: Monthly, quarterly, or upon receipt of new statements.

Financial Summaries

4

A Family Matter

4

Financial Summaries

Tab 4 continues the creative building of your Red Book. It gathers, in part, information from Tab 3, and requires the development of new documents to assist in the ongoing management of your estate.

The "Financial Summary" details the major components of your accumulated wealth. In addition to seeing assets as they change on a monthly basis you will use this information in Tab 7, Net Worth.

"Account Dividends" tracks, by equity, mutual fund, or other asset, the dividends earned over the course of a year. It can be used to see how successful you are this year, compare performance against last year, and check the tax information you receive at the conclusion of the year.

"Donations" tracks the charitable contributions you make during the year. Its primary value will be during preparation of your income tax return.

"Charitable Mileage" details the use of your privately owned vehicle in support of charitable activities. This will also prove useful during preparation of your income tax return.

"Stock Purchase Reconciliation" is designed to keep a running account of your stock buys and sells as they may occur. It will likely prove more useful than accumulating the confirmation orders provided by your brokerage firm. There is also benefit in that it may be used to check the accuracy of statements of recognized gains and losses you receive from your broker.

ACTION: Complete these documents using the sample formats provided and place into your Red Book as Tab 4.

UPDATE: Monthly or as significant events occur that impact or change this information.

Financial Summaries

FINANCIAL SUMMARY – ESTATE OF _____

for the year _____

	JAN VALUE	FEB VALUE	FEB CHANGE	MAR VALUE	MAR CHANGE	APR VALUE	APR CHANGE	MAY VALUE	MAY CHANGE	JUNE VALUE	JUNE CHANGE
Savings											
Checking											
Money Funds											
Equities											
Taxable Bonds											
Tax Exempt Bonds											
Mutual Funds											
Annuities											
Retirement Accounts											
TOTAL											
% MONTH CHANGE											
% YEAR CHANGE											

FINANCIAL SUMMARIES

JULY VALUE	JULY CHANGE	AUG VALUE	AUG CHANGE	SEP VALUE	SEP CHANGE	OCT VALUE	OCT CHANGE	NOV VALUE	NOV CHANGE	DEC VALUE	DEC CHANGE

A Family Matter

ACCOUNT			JAN	FEB	MAR	APR	MAY	JUN	JUL
STOCK									
	Name								
	Name								
	Name								
	Name								
	Name								
	Name								
	TOTAL 1		$ –	$ –	$ –	$ –	$ –	$ –	$ –
TAXABLE BONDS									
	TOTAL 2		$ –	$ –	$ –	$ –	$ –	$ –	$ –
TAX EXEMPT BONDS									
	TOTAL 3		$ –	$ –	$ –	$ –	$ –	$ –	$ –
MUTUAL FUNDS									
	TOTAL 4		$ –	$ –	$ –	$ –	$ –	$ –	$ –
ANNUITIES									
	TOTAL 5		$ –	$ –	$ –	$ –	$ –	$ –	$ –
MONEY FUND									
	TOTAL 6		$ –	$ –	$ –	$ –	$ –	$ –	$ –
RETIREMENT ACCOUNTS									
	TOTAL 7		$ –	$ –	$ –	$ –	$ –	$ –	$ –
TOTAL 8 (SUM 1 - 7)			$ –	$ –	$ –	$ –	$ –	$ –	$ –

ACCOUNT DIVIDENDS – ESTATE OF _____
for the year _____

Financial Summaries

	AUG	SEP	OCT	NOV	DEC
	$ –	$ –	$ –	$ –	$ –
	$ –	$ –	$ –	$ –	$ –
	$ –	$ –	$ –	$ –	$ –
	$ –	$ –	$ –	$ –	$ –
	$ –	$ –	$ –	$ –	$ –
	$ –	$ –	$ –	$ –	$ –
	$ –	$ –	$ –	$ –	$ –
	$ –	$ –	$ –	$ –	$ –

A Family Matter

DONATIONS – ESTATE OF _____
for the year _____

DATE	AGENCY	CHECK #	AMOUNT	REMARKS
		TOTAL	$ -	

Financial Summaries

| CHARITABLE MILEAGE – ESTATE OF _____ ||||
| for the year _____ ||||
DATE	AGENCY/PURPOSE	AMOUNT	REMARKS
	TOTAL	$ -	

STOCK PURCHASE RECONCILIATION – ESTATE OF _____
for the year _____

STOCK	DATE PURCHASED	PURCHASE PRICE	DATE SOLD	SOLD PRICE	PROFIT/ LOSS	REMARKS
TOTALS						

Retirement Statements

5

A Family Matter

5

Retirement Statements

Tab 5 gathers information concerning the status of your retirement accounts and/or participation in retirement programs. At a minimum, it should include a Social Security Personal Earnings and Benefit Statement (assuming you are paying, or have paid, into Social Security). This tab may also include:

- An account summary of your 401k, 403b, 457, or similar plan.

- The status of your participation in an Employee Stock Option Plan.

- A statement of your contributions and benefits in your employer's pension plan.

- A report on your Deferred Compensation Plan.

- A Retiree Account Statement (if you have reached this milestone in your life).

ACTION: Place these types of documents into your Red Book as Tab 5. If a Primary Beneficiary is not shown in the Retirement Statements, provide that information as part of Tab 5.

UPDATE: Quarterly or upon receipt of new statements.

Insurance

6

6

Insurance

Tab 6 gathers information pertaining to the various insurance policies you maintain on your home, your vehicles, and your life.

It may be useful to include here any policies you maintain for family members should the payment of premiums cease upon your incapacitation or demise.

Typical insurance policies include:

- Automobile/truck/RV insurance
- Home owner insurance
- Home/apartment renter insurance
- Health, vision, and dental insurance
- Whole life insurance
- Term life insurance
- Variable universal life insurance
- Long-term health care insurance
- Disability insurance

ACTION: Complete the information requested, using the sample format provided, and place into your Red Book as Tab 6.

UPDATE: As changes occur in your policy coverage or upon policy renewal or new policy purchase.

NOTE: It is absolutely essential that the location of each insurance policy be known by your personal representative, should you choose not to include it here.

INSURANCE – ESTATE OF _____
for the year _____

POLICY TYPE	AUTO	HOME	DENTAL	HEALTH	VISION	LIFE	LONG TERM	DISABILITY
POLICY NUMBER								
DATE PURCHASED								
FACE VALUE								
INSURED								
POLICY OWNER								
PRIMARY BENEFICIARY								
ALTERNATE BENEFICIARY								
COMPANY								
COMPANY CONTACT								
POLICY LOCATION								

A Family Matter

Net Worth

7

A Family Matter

7

Net Worth

Tab 7 gathers information with which you have calculated, or can calculate, your total net worth. It is an expansion of the Financial Portfolio Summary included in Tab 4 in that it includes your real and personal property as well as the value of insurance policies and other possessions.

There are three significant products in this tab:

- Net Worth Statement: the final product.

- Net Worth Back-up: this product details the several elements consolidated into the Net Worth Statement.

- Household Effects Inventory: this product identifies your furniture, appliance, houseware, and other personal possessions.

ACTION: Complete the three products using the sample formats provided and place into your Red Book as Tab 7. Recommend a videocassette also be made of the Household Effects Inventory and stored in a safe place such as a safe deposit box, a valuable asset should an insurance claim for loss be necessary.

UPDATE: As significant changes occur, at least annually to assist you in making/adjusting financial decisions or positions.

NET WORTH STATEMENT AS OF _____				
ESTATE OF _____				
ASSETS				**VALUE**
	Savings and Checking			
	Retirements Accounts			
	Investments			
	Cash Value Life Insurance			
	Real Estate			
	Receivables			
	Vehicles			
	Clothing			
	Furs and Jewelery			
	Kitchen and Housewares			
	Art and Pictures			
	Furniture			
	Appliances			
	Computers, Printers and Software			
	Books, Papers and Office Material			
	Recreational Equipment			
	Lawn and Garden			
	Linens and Curtains			
	Miscellaneous Household			
			TOTAL ASSETS	$ -
LIABILITIES				**VALUE**
	Real Estate Mortgage			
	Vehicle Loans			
	Personal Notes			
	Credit Cards			
			TOTAL LIABILITES	$ -
NET WORTH (Assets–Liabilities)				$ -

NET WORTH BACK-UP (SAMPLE)

ESTATE OF _____

ASSETS			VALUE
Savings and Checking			
	Cash		
	Checking		
	Savings		
	Money Market		
		Total	$ -
Investments			
	Equities		
	Taxable Bonds		
	Tax Exempt Bonds		
	Mutual Funds		
	Annuities		
		Total	$ -
Appliances			
	Refrigerator		
	Washer		
	Dryer		
	Dish Washer		
	Microwave Oven		
		Total	$ -
LIABILITIES			
Real Estate Mortgages			
	Principle Residence		
	Time Share		
		Total	$ -
Vehicles			
	99 Mercury		
	97 Cadillac		
		Total	$ -

A Family Matter

HOUSEHOLD EFFECTS INVENTORY AS OF _____ (SAMPLE)
ESTATE OF _____

ITEM	YEAR PURCHASED	ORIGINAL COST	MULTIPLIER **	CURRENT VALUE
Living Room	1986	$ 5,600.00	0.35	$ 1,960.00
Refrigerator*				
Master Bedroom				
Kitchen				
Writing Desk				
Piano				
Family Room				
Computer*				
Washer and Dryer*				
Living Room Chair				
Study				
Family Room Chairs				
TV				
Lawn Furniture*				
BBQ Grill*				
James Hagen Pix*				
Stained Glass*				
Wall Unit/Study				
Sofa and Love Seat				
Golf Clubs*				
VCR*				
Total				$ -

* Non-furniture item
** Mutiplier is a function of the depreciation method used to determine curent value

Income Tax Returns

8

A Family Matter

8

Income Tax Returns

Tab 8 gathers evidence to show that your Income Tax Returns were prepared for the two years prior to the current year. It may not be necessary to include all of the back-up schedules in this tab. If you choose not to, identify where they are located, so that your family and/or personal representative may find them.

If you are subject to a quarterly estimated tax payment, include a schedule of payment here to show the payments have been made.

ACTION: Place a copy of your Income Tax Returns (e.g., Forms 1040) for the last two years into your Red Book as Tab 8. Complete a schedule of payments using the sample format provided and include it as part of Tab 8.

UPDATE: Annually upon filing your tax return, quarterly when you pay your estimated tax payment.

RECORD OF ESTIMATED TAX PAYMENT
for the year _____

FEDERAL

Payment	Due Date	Amount Due	Amount Paid	Date Paid	Check Number
1					
2					
3					
4					
5					
6					
7					
8					
9					
10					
TOTAL		$ -	$ -		

STATE

Payment	Due Date	Amount Due	Amount Paid	Date Paid	Check Number
1					
2					
3					
4					
5					
6					
7					
8					
9					
10					
TOTAL		$ -	$ -		

Open Accounts

9

9

Open Accounts

Tab 9 gathers information on places where you do business. With this information, your personal representative will be able to ensure the businesses are contacted and that your accounts are paid and/or closed. The following accounts may be included in this tab:

- House Accounts: includes gas, electric, water, telephone, lawn service, security service, cable television, and pest control.

- Charge Accounts: includes bank cards, department store credit cards, gasoline credit cards, and business credit accounts.

- Subscriptions: includes newspapers, magazines, newsletters, and professional journals.

- Memberships: includes professional organizations, social/country clubs, record/movie/book clubs, fitness centers, airline/hotel reward programs, fraternal organizations, and civic clubs.

- Major Lump Sum Expenditures: includes those one-time expenditures for which special budgeting may be required, such as property taxes, long term health care premiums, contributions to church campaigns, and quarterly estimated tax payments.

A Family Matter

ACTION: Complete a listing for each of the accounts shown and place in your "Red Book" as Tab 9. For House Accounts, include the account number. For Charge Accounts include the account numbers on a copy of Tab 9 and keep in a secure location such as a safe deposit box. For subscriptions, include the expiration date.

UPDATE: As you add or delete accounts.

House Accounts (Account Number)

Charge Accounts (Account Number)

Subscriptions (Expiration Date)

Memberships

OPEN ACCOUNTS

MAJOR LUMP SUM EXPENDITURES			
PAYEE	AMOUNT	DUE DATE	REMARKS
Total	$ -		

A Family Matter

Safe Deposit Box Inventory

10

A Family Matter

10

Safe Deposit Box Inventory

Tab 10 gathers information on the contents of your safe deposit box, such that it can be used, if necessary, to determine the overall net worth of your estate. The following items may be included in this tab:

- Non-original copies of wills and powers of attorney
- Birth, marriage, divorce, adoption, and death certificates
- Automobile/truck/RV titles; lease agreements
- Home mortgages and deeds; lease contracts
- Listing of credit card and charge account numbers
- Stock and bond certificates; certificates of deposit
- Savings bonds
- Jewelry
- Cash (for an emergency or for use by your personal representative)
- Military discharge certificate

- Insurance policies

- Videocassette inventory of household effects and personal property

ACTION: Complete an inventory of your safe deposit box and place it in your Red Book as Tab 10. For items of significant value, include the cost or appraisal in the listing, or indicate the value is shown on a copy of the inventory in a secure location or in the safe deposit box.

UPDATE: As you put in or take out items from your safe deposit box; annually to ensure the inventory is current and accurate.

Information for Personal Representative

11

A Family Matter

11

Information for Personal Representative

Tab 11 gathers specific information you would like your personal representative to know as he/she undertakes the tasks necessary to close out your estate.

This information is equally valuable to your family during a life-threatening situation.

Items that may be included in this tab:

- Location of Important Documents: includes your wills, titles, mortgages, and other documents as shown.

- Advisors/Associates: includes your attorney, doctor, pastor, and other people as shown.

- Notifications: includes family, friends and business associates you would like to have informed in case of a life-threatening situation or upon your death.

- Personal Representative Checklist: Summarizes information pertaining to using the contents of this GUIDE and whatever special instructions you may have for your personal representative. Your attorney may also have this type of document to assist your personal representative.

A FAMILY MATTER

- Probate Information List: your attorney or your State Bar Association may have this type of document designed to assist you and your personal representative

ACTION: Complete the information as shown and include in your Red Book as Tab 11. Consult with your attorney as to the availability of a Personal Representative Checklist and/or Probate Information List; place in Tab 11.

UPDATE: As changes occur; review annually for accuracy.

Location of Important Documents

- Automobile and Other Titles:

- Bank Account Records:

- Bills and Payment Records: See Tab 9

- Birth Certificates:

- Burial Property Certificates/Instructions:

- Deeds/Release of Liens:

- Divorce Decree:

- Financial Statements/Accounting Records: See Tab 3

- Income Tax Returns for the Last 2 Years: See Tab 8

- Insurance Policies: See Tab 6

- Keys (House/Car/Truck/RV):

- Loan Documents:

- Marriage License:
- Military Discharge/ Separation Certificates:
- Mortgage Documents:
- Notice of Real Estate Appraised Value:
- Organ Donation Information: See Tab 12
- Prearranged Funeral Agreements:
- Retirement Plan Records: See Tab 5
- Royalty Agreements:
- Safe Deposit Box Key:
- Savings Bonds:
- Social Security Cards:
- Social Security Records: See Tab 5
- Stocks, Bonds and Securities: See Tab 3
- Wills/Powers of Attorney: See Tab 2

Advisors/Associates

1. Accountant:

2. Attorney:

3. Bank/Credit Union:

4. Dental Insurance:

5. Dentist:

6. Employer:

7. Financial Advisors:

8. Funeral Home:

9. Health Insurance:

10. Hospital:

11. Insurance:

12. OB-GYN:

13. Pastor:

14. Pharmacy:

15. Primary Care Physician:

16. Social Security Administration:

17. Specialist:

A Family Matter

Notifications

_____
_____
_____
_____
_____
_____
_____
_____
_____
_____
_____
_____
_____
_____
_____
_____
_____

The above named persons, in addition to those identified as Advisors/Associates, should be notified in the case of an emergency or life-threatening situation.

A Family Matter

Personal Representative Checklist

The following are typical items that you may want your personal representative to ensure are accomplished. Add or subtract from this list as you see fit. However, the specific timing of these items during the estate closing process is such that they should only be accomplished under the advice of your attorney.

1. Provide and/or review your Red Book with the attorney identified under Advisors/Associates and follow his or her advice and direction.

2. Notify all the persons shown under Notifications and as requested by the family.

3. Notify the appropriate organ donor agency.

4. Notify the funeral home either designated in Notifications or as selected by the family.

5. Follow burial instructions as specified in Location of Important Documents.

6. Obtain the original copy of all wills and powers of attorney if not held by the estate attorney.

7. Arrange an appropriate memorial service (personal/fraternal/military).

8. Place a notice in the obituary column of the local newspaper or as the family may request.

9. Identify all death benefits that would accrue to the family (employer/government/insurance).

10. Notify all businesses shown in Tab 9, Open Accounts.

11. Notify the U.S. Post Office and arrange for mail collection.

12. Obtain copies of the death certificate as directed by the estate attorney.

13. Ensure application for Social Security benefits is made.

14. Identify, oversee, and preserve the assets of the estate.

15. Verify contents of the safe deposit box shown in Tab 10.

16. Validate ownership of real property assets identified in Tab 7.

17. Validate the inventory of non-real property assets specified in Tab 7.

18. Process or assist in processing insurance claims.

19. Collect all debts owed and pay those debts (see Tab 9).

20. Sell assets of the estate as necessary to pay debts as well as income and death taxes.

21. Keep an accounting of all expenses incurred in closing the estate.

22. Prepare a final accounting of the estate.

23. File appropriate tax returns and pay all income and death taxes.

24. Request a closing letter from the Internal Revenue Service.

25. Distribute estate assets to identified beneficiaries.

26. Administer all matters pertaining to the comfort of the family and closure of the estate.

NOTE: These items are representative of the several activities with which I was involved in closing my mother's estate, many at the request of my attorney. I, therefore, strongly recommend, again, that you seek and heed the advice of your attorney as it relates to these items, as well as your other Advisors/Associates, as necessary, to complete this checklist.

A Family Matter

Miscellaneous

12

A Family Matter

12

Miscellaneous

Tab 12 gathers information which does not fit in other tabs, but that you believe would be of value to your family, to your personal representative, or to meeting the purposes stated in this GUIDE. Items that may be included:

- Pending Changes/Updates to your Red Book
- Organ donor cards
- Children's Social Security account numbers
- Military Retiree Casualty Assistance checklist
- Newspaper/periodical articles concerning Red Book matters

ACTION: Place the appropriate documents in Tab 12; complete the Pending Changes/Updates format as needed.

UPDATE: As required

NOTE: The Pending Changes/Updates to your "Red Book" format may be useful to record an activity such as a purchase you will later include in your Net Worth statement when you update it, or to just hold information for future reference.

TAB	Change/Update	Posted	Remarks

Your Personal Red Book

A Family Matter

The Estate of

_____

This page starts Your Personal Red Book; the gathering of that essential information capable of defining your future and that of your family. The several formats and spreadsheets shown throughout the book are summarized in the Appendix. The Formats are in Microsoft Word and the Spreadsheets are in Microsoft Excel.

Notwithstanding, please develop your personal Red Book in a style and format, and with that information, that best serves your individual needs, as well as the purposes stated at the outset.

And then, What's Next?

A Family Matter

Next!

Congratulations! Now, where do you go from here?

Now that you have gathered all the information suggested in this GUIDE, SHARE IT!

Share the information with your family, your attorney, your accountant, your financial advisors, and most assuredly with your personal representative. Certainly, it may not be necessary to share every detail (i.e., you may want to keep your financial summary confidential).

But, what is important is to share the existence of the completed document, your Red Book, as well as its location.

Of equal importance is to keep the information current. Some information changes monthly; other information less frequently. Keeping your Red Book current ensures each of the stated purposes of this GUIDE will be met and your family will be forever grateful.

Again, congratulations!

A Family Matter

Thanks!

I am not an attorney specializing in estate planning. I am not a financial planner with several suffixes behind my name. And I am not an insurance agent or equities broker focusing on sales and earnings.

What I am is a person who believes in organization, putting "things" in the right place, so as we need them they are there, available to serve us. I owe that to my family, and respectfully suggest that if you have come this far in this GUIDE, you agree your family deserves it too!

I trust you have benefited from developing your personal Red Book and that you and your family will continue to do so.

Thanks!

A Family Matter

Appendix

Formats and Spreadsheets

Capturing all the information gathered for your personal Red Book.

    The Estate of

    Tab Index

    Tab 1 Principal Profile Cover Sheet

    Principal Profile Spreadsheet

    Tab 2 Wills/Powers of Attorney Cover Sheet

    Tab 3 Investment Accounts Cover Sheet

    Tab 4 Financial Summaries Cover Sheet

    Financial Summary Spreadsheet

    Account Dividends Spreadsheet

    Donations Spreadsheet

    Charitable Mileage Spreadsheet

Stock Purchase Reconciliation Spreadsheet

Tab 5 Retirement Statements Cover Sheet

Tab 6 Insurance Cover Sheet

Insurance Spreadsheet

Tab 7 Net Worth Cover Sheet

Net Worth Statement Spreadsheet

Net Worth Backup Spreadsheet

Household Effects Inventory Spreadsheet

Tab 8 Income Tax Returns Cover Sheet

Record of Estimated Tax Payment Spreadsheet

Tab 9 Open Accounts Cover Sheet

Open Accounts Formats

Major Lump Sum Expenditures Spreadsheet

Tab 10 Safe Deposit Box Inventory Cover Sheet

Tab 11 Information for Personal Representative Cover Sheet

Location of Important Documents Format

Advisors/Associates Format

Notifications Format

Tab 12 Miscellaneous Cover Sheet

Pending Changes/Updates to the "Red Book" Spreadsheet

Biography

WILLIAM A. VERKEST

A husband, father, grandfather, professional engineer, and retired senior United States Air Force officer, who believes his many personal and professional successes have resulted from an inherent ability to "organize"—from the simple project through the complex organization. In *A Family Matter*, he blends this talent with the experience he gained from being solely responsible for closing his mother's estate. The result is an exceptional layperson-to-layperson discussion of a subject immensely important to all families.